2013?

A DOOMSDAY DAY PLANNER

2013?: A DOOMSDAY DAY PLANNER

by Mark Hagen

ISBN 978-0-9852044-2-6

DESIGN Jessica Fleischmann / still room, with Mark Hagen

PRODUCTION ASSISTANT Robyn Baker

PUBLISHED BY International Art Objects Galleries, Los Angeles; Almine Rech Gallery, Paris and Brussels; Paper Chase Press, Los Angeles

NAME ______________________________

ADDRESS ___________________________

____

MOBILE PHONE ______________________

LAND LINE _________________________

EMAIL _____________________________

BLOOD TYPE ________________________

ALLERGIES _________________________

____

____

EMERGENCY CONTACTS

NAME ______________________________

MOBILE PHONE ______________________

EMAIL _____________________________

RELATION __________________________

LAND LINE _________________________

NAME ______________________________

MOBILE PHONE ______________________

EMAIL _____________________________

RELATION __________________________

LAND LINE _________________________

POLICE DEPT. ______________________

FIRE DEPT. ________________________

HOSPITAL __________________________

UTILITIES _________________________

JANUARY 2013?

MONDAY	TUESDAY	WEDNESDAY	THURSDAY	FRIDAY	SATURDAY / SUNDAY
	1	2	3	4	5
					6
7	8	9	10	11	12
					13
14	15	16	17	18	19
					20
21	22	23	24	25	26
					27
28	29	30	31		

FEBRUARY 2013?

MONDAY	TUESDAY	WEDNESDAY	THURSDAY	FRIDAY	SATURDAY / SUNDAY
				1	2
					3
4	5	6	7	8	9
					10
11	12	13	14	15	16
					17
18	19	20	21	22	23
					24
25	26	27	28		

MARCH 2013?

MONDAY	TUESDAY	WEDNESDAY	THURSDAY	FRIDAY	SATURDAY / SUNDAY
				1	2 / 3
4	5	6	7	8	9 / 10
11	12	13	14	15	16 / 17
18	19	20	21	22	23 / 24
25	26	27	28	29	30 / 31

MONDAY	TUESDAY	WEDNESDAY	THURSDAY	FRIDAY	SATURDAY / SUNDAY
1	2	3	4	5	6 / 7
8	9	10	11	12	13 / 14
15	16	17	18	19	20 / 21
22	23	24	25	26	27 / 28
29	30				

MAY 2013?

MONDAY	TUESDAY	WEDNESDAY	THURSDAY	FRIDAY	SATURDAY / SUNDAY
		1	2	3	4 / 5
6	7	8	9	10	11 / 12
13	14	15	16	17	18 / 19
20	21	22	23	24	25 / 26
27	28	29	30	31	

MONDAY	TUESDAY	WEDNESDAY	THURSDAY	FRIDAY	SATURDAY / SUNDAY
					1
					2
3	4	5	6	7	8
					9
10	11	12	13	14	15
					16
17	18	19	20	21	22
					23
24	25	26	27	28	29
					30

JULY 2013?

MONDAY	TUESDAY	WEDNESDAY	THURSDAY	FRIDAY	SATURDAY / SUNDAY
1	2	3	4	5	6 7
8	9	10	11	12	13 14
15	16	17	18	19	20 21
22	23	24	25	26	27 28
29	30	31			

MONDAY	TUESDAY	WEDNESDAY	THURSDAY	FRIDAY	SATURDAY / SUNDAY
			1	2	3 / 4
5	6	7	8	9	10 / 11
12	13	14	15	16	17 / 18
19	20	21	22	23	24 / 25
26	27	28	29	30	31 /

SEPTEMBER 2013?

MONDAY	TUESDAY	WEDNESDAY	THURSDAY	FRIDAY	SATURDAY / SUNDAY
					1
2	3	4	5	6	7 / 8
9	10	11	12	13	14 / 15
16	17	18	19	20	21 / 22
23	24	25	26	27	28 / 29
30					

MONDAY	TUESDAY	WEDNESDAY	THURSDAY	FRIDAY	SATURDAY / SUNDAY
	1	2	3	4	5
					6
7	8	9	10	11	12
					13
14	15	16	17	18	19
					20
21	22	23	24	25	26
					27
28	29	30	31		

NOVEMBER 2013?

MONDAY	TUESDAY	WEDNESDAY	THURSDAY	FRIDAY	SATURDAY / SUNDAY
				1	2
					3
4	5	6	7	8	9
					10
11	12	13	14	15	16
					17
18	19	20	21	22	23
					24
25	26	27	28	29	30

DECEMBER 2013?

MONDAY	TUESDAY	WEDNESDAY	THURSDAY	FRIDAY	SATURDAY / SUNDAY
					1
2	**3**	**4**	**5**	**6**	**7** / **8**
9	**10**	**11**	**12**	**13**	**14** / **15**
16	**17**	**18**	**19**	**20**	**21** / **22**
23	**24**	**25**	**26**	**27**	**28** / **29**
30	**31**				

DECEMBER 2012/JANUARY 2013?

31 MONDAY

1 TUESDAY

2 WEDNESDAY

January 1, 2000
Filipino religious leader Cerferino Quinte prophesied an "all-consuming rain of fire" would destroy the world on January 1, 2000. In preparation, he and his followers built the Tunnels of Salvation, a series of bomb shelters large enough to accommodate more than 700 people, stockpiled with a year's worth of provisions.

January 1, 2000
In 1998, the American authors of the best-selling Left Behind series of apocalyptic fiction, Tim LaHaye and Jerry Jenkins, prophesied that the Y2K bug at the start of the year 2000 would trigger a global "financial meltdown," allowing the "Antichrist or his emissaries…to dominate the world commercially."

1st Century CE The apostles and earliest members of Jesus' apocalyptic Jewish sect expected his Second Coming in their lifetime, during the first century of the common era.

70 The Essenes of Roman Judaea believed they were the "last generation of the last generations" and that the Jewish revolt against the Romans in 66–70 was the final end-time battle.

NOTES

3 THURSDAY

4 FRIDAY

5 SATURDAY

6 SUNDAY

JANUARY 2013?

7 MONDAY

8 TUESDAY

9 WEDNESDAY

January 9, 1951
Pentecostal religious leader Grace Agnes Carlson, who went by the name Elect Gold, and her followers, The Children of Light, wore white robes and held a 15-day vigil on a farm in British Columbia in preparation for the end of the world on January 9, 1951, as prophesied by Carlson.

10 THURSDAY

11 FRIDAY

12 SATURDAY

13 SUNDAY

January 1974
In 1968 in Huntington Beach, California, David Brandt Berg, also known as Moses David, founded the Children of God, famous for its practice of "flirty fishing," or using female members to seduce new converts. Berg made several predictions, the most famous being that in January 1974 the comet Kohoutek would cause economic collapse and the "total downfall of America".

2nd Century Self-proclaimed prophet Montanus, founder of an early Christian sect called the New Prophecy, believed that Jesus would return in his lifetime—during the second century—to found a New Jerusalem in what is now modern-day Turkey. Members of the New Prophecy church were declared heretics by the proto-orthodox Church for their ecstatic "speaking in tongues" and their recognition of female bishops.

380 The Donatists, members of a Christian sect in Roman North Africa, predicted the world would end in 380.

JANUARY 2013?

14 MONDAY

15 TUESDAY

16 WEDNESDAY

17 THURSDAY

NOTES

18 FRIDAY

19 SATURDAY

20 SUNDAY

Late 4th Century In his *Contra Constantium Augustum Liber*, written in 365, Bishop Hilary of Poitiers declared that the recently deceased Roman Emperor Constantius II had been the Antichrist.

Late 4th Century The French bishop Martin of Tours announced in 389, eight years before his death, that the Antichrist had been born and that "he will, after reaching maturity, achieve supreme power."

JANUARY 2013?

21 MONDAY

22 TUESDAY

23 WEDNESDAY

24 THURSDAY

NOTES

25 FRIDAY

26 SATURDAY

27 SUNDAY

5th Century In the fifth century, apocalyptic prophet Moses of Crete claimed to be the Jewish Messiah and promised to part the Mediterranean Sea and lead his followers back to Jerusalem. His followers purportedly abandoned their possessions and gathered on the promised day, casting themselves into the sea at his command.

500 In the early third century, Christian historian Sextus Julius Africanus used Christian scripture to calculate the period between creation and Jesus' birth, arriving at the figure of 5,500 years. Then he predicted that the end-time would occur in the year 500, or 6,000 years after creation.

JANUARY 2013?

28 MONDAY

29 TUESDAY

30 WEDNESDAY

31 THURSDAY

NOTES

1 FRIDAY

2 SATURDAY

3 SUNDAY

500 Hippolytus, the third-century theologian of the Roman Church, proclaimed in one of his many writings devoted to apocalyptic themes that Christ would return in the year 500, calculated to be 6,000 years after creation.

590 The French bishop Gregory of Tours wrote in his *History of the Franks* that in the year 590, famine, disease, and the appearance of several false prophets, including the false Christ of Bourges, were signs of the end-time as predicted in the Gospels. The false Christ of Bourges, who had amassed a following of more than 3,000 people, some of them Church clergy, was eventually "cut into bits" in front of his followers on the orders of Bishop Aurelius.

FEBRUARY 2013?

4 MONDAY

5 TUESDAY

6 WEDNESDAY

7 THURSDAY

NOTES

8 FRIDAY

9 SATURDAY

10 SUNDAY

Late 6th Century Pope Gregory I sent the first Christian missionaries to England in 596 to prepare for the end-time, declaring that "the world grows old and hoary and hastens to its approaching end."

800 The occupation of what is now Spain by Arabian Muslims from North Africa coupled with the belief that the bishop of Toledo was the Antichrist prompted Asturian monk Beatus of Liébana to predict in his 776 *Commentary on the Apocalypse* that the end-time was at hand and the apocalypse would begin in the year 800.

FEBRUARY 2013?

11 MONDAY

12 TUESDAY

13 WEDNESDAY

14 THURSDAY

February 14, 1420
Martin Huska, of the radical Christian Taborite movement, known for its anti–Roman Catholic Church views, claimed Prague was Babylon and told his followers to abandon it because Christ was to establish his millennial kingdom on earth and punish all sinners by February 14, 1420.

February 14, 1891
On February 14, 1835, New England religious leader and founder of the Latter Day Saint movement Joseph Smith prophesied "the coming of the Lord, which is nigh, even 56 years should wind up the scene." Previously, in 1823, Smith claimed that an angel named Moroni revealed to him the location of ancient golden plates and a set of silver spectacles equipped with two seer stone lenses named Urim and Thummim. These spectacles allowed Smith to read and translate the "reformed Egyptian" inscribed on the plates into his 1830 Book of Mormon.

NOTES

15 FRIDAY

16 SATURDAY

17 SUNDAY

847 In the German city of Mainz, the self-proclaimed prophetess Thiota said that God told her the world would end in 847. Both commoners and priests followed her until she was arrested by the archbishop Rabanus Maurus and publicly flogged.

1000 At the turn of the first millennium, English priest and monk Byrhtferth declared, "The Satanic number 1,000 has been reached" and that the Savior would soon "complete the count of years."

FEBRUARY 2013?

18 MONDAY

19 TUESDAY

20 WEDNESDAY

21 THURSDAY

February 20, 1524

In 1499, German mathematician, astrologer, and priest Johannes Stöffler saw the planetary alignments in Pisces of this year as a sign that a flood would destroy the world. Convinced, Count von Iggleheim constructed a three-story ark on the Rhine. As rain began to fall on the designated day—February 20, 1524—a crowd of people hoping for a seat on the ark began to riot. Hundreds were killed, including the count. Stöffler later recalculated his doomsday date to be in 1528.

NOTES

22 FRIDAY

23 SATURDAY

24 SUNDAY

1000 Numerous Christian authorities, including Pope Sylvester II, expected the Second Coming of Jesus Christ in the year 1000.

1027 In Aquitaine, France, rumors of a "rain of blood that could not be washed off," which coincided with the return of French pilgrims from Jerusalem, persuaded the entire region that the apocalypse would occur in 1027.

FEBRUARY 2013?

25 MONDAY

26 TUESDAY

27 WEDNESDAY

28 THURSDAY

February 28, 1761
Englishman George (John) Bell, also known as the Life Guardsman, predicted the end of the world or at least the destruction of London by earthquake on February 28, 1761. Bell was also known for his miracle healings and to have attempted to restore a blind man's sight by touching his eyes with spittle and pronouncing the word *ephphatha*.

1 FRIDAY

2 SATURDAY

3 SUNDAY

1033 Various Christian chroniclers believed 1033 to be the year of the first millennium—the 1000th anniversary of the death and resurrection of Jesus Christ—and that the end of the world was imminent.

1033 Claiming that the Antichrist had been born in the year 1000 and citing divine omens in the form of famines, eclipses, and plagues 33 years later, Burgundy monk Rodulfus Glaber announced that "Satan would be unleashed" in 1033.

4 MONDAY	**5** TUESDAY	**6** WEDNESDAY	**7** THURSDAY

NOTES

8 FRIDAY

9 SATURDAY

10 SUNDAY

March 10, 1982
In 1974, English doctor of astrophysics and science writer John Gribbin coauthored, with Stephen Plagemann, the book *The Jupiter Effect*. In it, they claimed that on March 10, 1982, an alignment of planets would change the speed of the earth's rotation and orbit, causing global catastrophe, including the destruction of Los Angeles by earthquake.

Late 11th–Early 12th Century Pope Urban II launched the First Crusade in 1095 to help Christianity "flourish again in these last times, so that when Antichrist begins his reign there, as he shortly must, he will find enough Christians to fight."

Late 11th–Early 12th Century Guibert of Nogent, a Benedictine historian and theologian, described the first crusades (from 1095 to 1099) to Jerusalem in his book *The Deeds of God Through the Franks* as a necessary prelude to an imminent end-time war with the Antichrist.

March 1899
In 1891, Yale University military instructor Charles Adelle Lewis Totten's study of biblical chronology, prophecy, and the "secret messages" encoded in the Great Pyramid at Giza led him to predict that the end of the world would come in March 1899. Totten was also an ardent proponent of British Israelism, or the belief that the people of Great Britain are the descendants of the ten lost tribes of Israel.

MARCH 2013?

11 MONDAY

12 TUESDAY

13 WEDNESDAY

14 THURSDAY

NOTES

15 FRIDAY

16 SATURDAY

17 SUNDAY

March 16, 2880
Scientists suggest that if the 1.4-kilometer-wide, near-earth asteroid (29075) 1950 DA continues on its present course, it would approach the earth on March 16, 2880, with an possible impact probability of 1 in 300. The energy released by a collision with 1950 DA would have dramatic effects on the climate, devastating the biosphere and human civilization.

1260 Joachim of Fiore, founder of the Abbey of Fiora in the mountains of Calabria, Italy, was a theologian, writer, and interpreter of the Book of Revelation. In his 1195 *Expositio in Apocalypsim*, he predicted that the "age of the Holy Spirit" would begin by 1260, making the Church unnecessary. Pope Alexander IV declared him a heretic in 1263.

1260 Gerard of Borgo San Donnino, a Sicilian-born friar living in Paris, believed that Joachim of Fiore was not only a prophet but in fact the angel of the apocalypse. In 1250, he published his *Introductorium in Evangelium Aeternum*, which stated that in 1260 an "Order of Justs" would come rule the Roman Catholic Church. In 1263, Gerard was sentenced to life in prison.

March 1928
In his 1896 publication titled *The Appointed Time: Being Scriptural, Historical, and Astronomical Proofs of the End of the Gentile Times in 1898 1/4 and the coming of the Lord*, English writer Jabez Bunting Dimbleby predicted, through complicated biblical chronology, that March 1898 would be the beginning of the Great Tribulation and March 1928 the beginning of Christ's millennium.

18 MONDAY

19 TUESDAY

20 WEDNESDAY

21 THURSDAY

March 21, 1844
In 1818, after extensive biblical calculation, New England preacher William Miller, leader of the Millerite movement, predicted that Jesus Christ would return between March 21, 1843, and March 21, 1844. He amassed a following of thousands.

22 FRIDAY

23 SATURDAY

24 SUNDAY

1279 In 1213, Pope Innocent III launched the Fifth Crusade with: "We nevertheless put our trust in the Lord who has already given us a sign that good is to come, that the end of this beast [Islam] is approaching, whose number, according to the Revelation of St. John, will end in 666 years, of which already nearly 600 have passed."

1368 Spanish physician and alchemist Arnaldus de Villa Nova, who is famous for discovering carbon monoxide and pure alcohol, wrote in his 1300 *Tractatus de Tempore Adventu Antichristi* that the Antichrist would come in 1368.

25 MONDAY · **26** TUESDAY · **27** WEDNESDAY · **28** THURSDAY

March 25, 992
Biblical chronologists from Lotharingia (modern-day central Europe) circulated a prediction that the end-time would begin on March 25, 992, when both the feast of the Annunciation and Good Friday fell.

March 25, 1985
In 1983, Vern Bennom Grimsley, author and preacher in the Urantia movement, based around the anonymous, 2,097-page *Urantia Book*, which surfaced in Chicago sometime between 1924 and 1955, prophesied that World War III would begin on March 25, 1985. In anticipation, he and his followers built a bomb shelter near San Francisco, while fellow Urantian community member John Hay, cofounder of Celestial Seasonings Tea, spent $2 million converting a cave in Arkansas into a lavish bomb shelter.

29 FRIDAY

30 SATURDAY

31 SUNDAY

1370 French friar and alchemist Jean de Roquetaillade foresaw in his 1356 *Vademecum in Tribulatione*, imminent tribulations where the "lay and oppressed peoples will rebel…and take the temporal goods away from the clergy," culminating in the arrival of two Antichrists by 1370.

Late 14th Century Popular belief held that the black plague, which spread across Europe from 1346 to 1351, was the first major sign of the end of times.

APRIL 2013?

1 MONDAY

2 TUESDAY

3 WEDNESDAY

4 THURSDAY

April 1, 1780
Rhode Island Quaker Jemima Wilkinson claimed in 1776, after a lingering illness, that she had died and been reborn as the "Publick Universal Friend," a messenger of God. Shortly after, she formed the Society of Universal Friends, which practiced communal living and equality of the sexes in frontier New York. Wilkinson predicted the millennium would occur on April 1, 1780.

5 FRIDAY

6 SATURDAY

7 SUNDAY

April 5, 1534
German Anabaptist Jan Matthys, leader of the Münster Rebellion, predicted that the "judgment of the wicked" would take place on April 5, 1534, when Easter Day fell, and only the city of Münster, which the Anabaptists had taken control of, would be spared. Instead, Matthys was murdered by Roman Catholic Church loyalists, who placed his head on a pole just outside the city.

Late 14th Century
Archdeacon Jan Milíč of Kroměříž, of present-day Czech Republic, claimed that the Antichrist had come and that the end-time was near. In 1367, he went to Rome to preach this belief but was thrown into prison by the Inquisition.

1525 According to German Radical Reformation preacher Thomas Müntzer, 1525 would be the beginning of Christ's millennium. Müntzer led a battle in May 1525 during the unsuccessful Peasants' War (1524–25) against nobles loyal to the Roman Catholic Church. Defeated, Müntzer was subsequently captured, tortured, and beheaded.

APRIL 2013?

8 MONDAY

9 TUESDAY

10 WEDNESDAY

11 THURSDAY

NOTES

12 FRIDAY

13 SATURDAY

14 SUNDAY

1528 In 1528, German furrier Hans Römer, who had taken part in the failed Peasants' War, urged peasants to revolt against "godless authorities" as the world was to be completely destroyed by an earthquake within one year. On New Year's Day 1528, he and his fellow Anabaptists conspired unsuccessfully to take over the city of Erfurt to turn it into a New Jerusalem.

Mid-16th Century Bishop of Vienna Friedrich Nausea cited rumors of "monstrous births" and "prodigiorum," or wonders in the sky, as omens of the imminent end of the world in his 1532 *Libri Mirabilium Septem.*

APRIL 2013?

15 MONDAY

16 TUESDAY

17 WEDNESDAY

18 THURSDAY

April 18, 1844
After New England preacher William Miller's first prediction for the return of Jesus Christ between March 21, 1843 and March 21, 1844, failed, he revised his date to April 18, 1844.

NOTES

19 FRIDAY

20 SATURDAY

21 SUNDAY

April 21, 633 BCE Many Romans feared that the 12 eagles that legend said had appeared to Romulus at Rome's founding on April 21, 753 BCE, symbolized one decade of existence each and that their city would be destroyed exactly 120 years later in 633.

1533 German Anabaptist preacher Melchior Hoffman of northern Germany predicted that 1533 was the year of Christ's Second Coming, that Strasbourg was to be the seat of the New Jerusalem, and that the return of Christ would be preceded by a purging of the ungodly. This prediction inspired the Münster Rebellion, for which he was imprisoned for life.

1537 In 1531, Dijon astrologer Pierre Turrel calculated in his *The Period, That Is to Say, the End of the World*, four different possible dates in which the world would be destroyed by the Antichrist's "rain of fire": 1537, 1544, 1801, and 1814.

22 MONDAY

23 TUESDAY

24 WEDNESDAY

25 THURSDAY

April 22, 1959
Florence Houteff, widow of religious leader, author, and illustrator Victor Tasho Houteff, claimed that the 42 months prophesied in Revelation would begin in early 1956 and end with the Rapture on April 22, 1959. Hundreds gathered with her outside Waco, Texas, not far from the headquarters of the Davidian Seventh-day Adventist Church, which Victor Houteff had established after being excommunicated from the Seventh-day Adventist Church in Los Angeles. The Seventh-day Adventist Church itself grew out of the Millerite movement of the 1840s.

April 23, 1990
In 1986, Elizabeth Clare Prophet, leader of the New Age group The Church Universal and Triumphant, and self-proclaimed Vicar of Christ, "karma-free" Bodhisattva, and reincarnation of both Nefertiti and the high priestess of Atlantis, claimed "Ascended Masters" had revealed to her that a global nuclear war would happen on April 23, 1990. She and her followers would go on to build a 750-person underground shelter on their 7,000-acre compound in Montana.

NOTES

26 FRIDAY

27 SATURDAY

28 SUNDAY

April 28, 1583
London astrologer Richard Harvey circulated pamphlets that claimed that the conjunction of the "superiour planets Saturne & Jupiter" in Pisces on April 28, 1583, would result in a world-destroying flood.

1584 The conjunction of nearly all the planets in Aries in 1584 led Bohemian (present-day Czech Republic) astrologer Cyprian Leowitz to conclude that it "undoubtedly announces the Second Coming of the son of God."

1588 In the 15th century, German mathematician and astronomer Regiomontanus (Johannes Müller von Königsberg) prophesied that planetary alignments and eclipses in 1588 would cause empires to collapse and the whole world to suffer upheavals.

APRIL/MAY 2013?

29 MONDAY

30 TUESDAY

1 WEDNESDAY

April 29, 1980
Leland Jensen, doctor of chiropractics and natural medicine, and founder of the Bahá'ís Under the Provisions of the Covenant, a Montana-based splinter sect of the Bahá'í Faith (the monotheistic religion founded by Bahá'u'lláh in 19th-century Persia), predicted that "either a provocative act that will escalate into World War III, or World War III itself" was to occur on April 29, 1980, at 5:55 p.m. He later predicted that Halley's comet would collide with the earth on April 29, 1987.

NOTES

2 THURSDAY

3 FRIDAY

4 SATURDAY

5 SUNDAY

May 5, 2001
Gabriel of Urantia, born Tony Delevin, leader and founder of the Sedona, Arizona-based, UFO-focused New Age group Aquarian Concepts Community, claimed that "earth changes" and "distortion waves" would destroy humanity between the dates of May 5, 2000, and May 5, 2001. Delevin also claimed to be an Audio Fusion Material Complement, or a channeler of "celestial personalities" who would bring a group of alien spaceships to save the members of his group before the earth's destruction.

MAY 2013?

6 MONDAY

7 TUESDAY

8 WEDNESDAY

9 THURSDAY

NOTES

10 FRIDAY

11 SATURDAY

12 SUNDAY

1600 In 1598, Italian theologian, astrologer, and philosopher Tommaso Campanella held that the prophecies of Joachim of Fiore, along with his own astrological observations, foresaw the coming of the "age of the spirit" in the year 1600. Incarcerated shortly thereafter for conspiring to overthrow Spanish rule and establish a communistic commonwealth in his hometown of Stilo, Campanella was imprisoned and tortured, only to be released 27 years later by Pope Urban VIII to become his astrological advisor.

MAY 2013?

13 MONDAY

14 TUESDAY

15 WEDNESDAY

16 THURSDAY

May 15, 2003
Yuko Chino, self-proclaimed prophet and leader of the Japanese New Age religious group Pana-Wave Laboratory —whose members dressed in all white and caravanned around the country in an attempt to evade "scalar electromagnetic waves"— claimed that on May 15, 2003, the nearby passing of an undiscovered tenth planet would cause the earth's axis to flip and lead to catastrophic earthquakes and tsunamis that would destroy most of humanity.

17 FRIDAY

18 SATURDAY

19 SUNDAY

1614 German physician and astrologer Helisaeus Roeslin's analysis of the Bible; the sequence of European popes, emperors, and kings; and the conjunctures of planets in the zodiac, as well as the nova star of 1572 and the comet of 1577, led him to predict in his 1579 *Speculum Mundi* that Christ's millennial New Age would begin in 1614.

1653 The Fifth Monarchy Men, a radical sect of English Puritans, saw the overthrow and beheading of King Charles I at the hands of Oliver Cromwell as a necessary precursor to Christ's Second Coming. Cromwell's establishment of the Nominated Assembly in 1653, of which some delegates were Fifth Monarchy members, was seen to indicate that the "rule of the saints" had begun.

MAY 2013?

20 MONDAY

21 TUESDAY

22 WEDNESDAY

23 THURSDAY

May 21, 2011
American preacher and Christian radio broadcaster Harold Egbert Camping's second prediction date was May 21, 2011, for the return of Jesus Christ and the rapture of 200 million people. Hundreds of his followers quit their jobs and participated in a million-dollar campaign to spread his message of humanity's imminent demise. On June 9, 2011, Camping suffered a stroke and was hospitalized.

24 FRIDAY

25 SATURDAY

26 SUNDAY

1657 Explorer, colonizer, and navigator Christopher Columbus wrote in his 1502 *Book of Prophecies* that the world was created in 5343 BCE and would last 7,000 years, thus ending in 1657. With the end-time looming, Columbus hoped that the gold brought back from the New World would finance a final Spanish-led crusade to recapture Jerusalem.

1666 The year 1666 being a combination of the millennium and the number of the beast, coupled with the catastrophic events of the Great Plague of London (1664–66) and the Great Fire of London in September 1666, convinced many Londoners that their fears of the end of the world had been realized.

MAY 2013?

27 MONDAY | **28** TUESDAY | **29** WEDNESDAY | **30** THURSDAY

May 27, 1528

The German Radical Reformation preacher Hans Hut predicted the final purification of the world for May 27, 1528, when Pentecost fell. In 1527, Hut was arrested for heresy as well as for his role in the Peasants' War, during which he preached that "subjects should murder all the authorities, for the opportune time has arrived." He died from asphyxiation when a fire broke out in his prison. The next day, his dead body was burned at the stake.

May 27, 2003

In 1995, Nancy Lieder, a self-proclaimed alien contactee and channeler of Zetans (aliens from the star Zeta Reticuli), claimed that a "Planet X" would come closest to the earth on May 27, 2003, causing a physical pole shift as well as the destruction of all civilization. In a radio interview one week before this date, Lieder also claimed that she had euthanized her pets in anticipation of doomsday and suggested others to do the same.

May 29, 1928

In 1924, English physician and pyramidologist Dr. Herbert Aldersmith coauthored, with the Scottish engineer David Davidson, the exhaustive book *The Great Pyramid: Its Divine Message*. Aldersmith believed that the Great Pyramid of Giza was a chronological map to the dates of the Second Coming and end-time, which, according to his calculations, was to start May 29, 1928.

NOTES

31 FRIDAY

1 SATURDAY

2 SUNDAY

1673 William Aspinwall, a member of the Fifth Monarchy movement, wrote in his tract *A brief Description of the Fifth Monarchy, or Kingdom That Is Shortly to Come into the World* that the "Antichrist's dominion will be in the year 1673."

1688 John Napier of Merchiston, a Scottish mathematician, physicist, astronomer, and astrologer, wrote in his 1594 *A Plaine Discovery of the Whole Revelation of St. John* that after a numerological analysis of the Book of Revelation, he predicted that the apocalypse would occur in 1688 or 1700.

JUNE 2013?

3 MONDAY

4 TUESDAY

5 WEDNESDAY

6 THURSDAY

NOTES

7 FRIDAY

8 SATURDAY

9 SUNDAY

1689 French Protestant leader Pierre Jurieu claimed in his 1686 *Accomplissement des Propheties* that the overthrow of the pope, who was the Antichrist, would take place in 1689.

1694 English Nonconformist Protestant pastor John Mason preached in 1690 that the Second Coming of Christ was imminent and that it would take place in Water Stratford in 1694. Believing Mason a prophet and that everywhere else would be destroyed, hundreds of people sold their possessions and moved there between the fall of 1693 and Easter 1694. Mason died of a quinsy in May of 1694.

JUNE 2013?

10 MONDAY

11 TUESDAY

12 WEDNESDAY

13 THURSDAY

NOTES

14 FRIDAY

15 SATURDAY

16 SUNDAY

Fall 1694 German radical theologian, mathematician, and astronomer Johann Jacob Zimmerman claimed in his *Muthmassliche Zeit-Bestimmung* that the apocalypse would occur in the fall of 1694. With this in mind, Zimmermann planned to lead his followers to North America to build a "Society of the Woman in the Wilderness." He died, however, just before their planned departure.

1697 For colonial New England's foremost theologian, historian, Puritan minister, and witch hunter, Cotton Mather, the persecution of Protestants in France, the rampant witchcraft in Salem, and the earthquakes of the late 17th century all marked the "Millennium's opening." Mather predicted 1697 as the year of Christ's Second Coming; he would later revise this date to 1716 and then again to 1736.

JUNE 2013?

17 MONDAY

18 TUESDAY

19 WEDNESDAY

20 THURSDAY

NOTES

21 FRIDAY

22 SATURDAY

23 SUNDAY

1700 In his 1642 pamphlet, *The Personal Reign of Christ Upon Earth*, Henry Archer, of the Fifth Monarchy movement, predicted the Jews of the world would be converted to Christianity by 1656 and that in 1700 Christ would return.

1757 In his 1758 book titled *The Last Judgment and Babylon Destroyed. All the Predictions in the Apocalypse Are at This Day Fulfilled*, Swedish scientist, philosopher, Christian mystic, and vegetarian Emanuel Swedenborg claimed that the Last Judgment had already occurred in 1757, although only in the spiritual world.

JUNE 2013?

24 MONDAY

25 TUESDAY

26 WEDNESDAY

27 THURSDAY

NOTES

28 FRIDAY

29 SATURDAY

30 SUNDAY

June 28, 1981
Reverend Bill Maupin, founder of Lighthouse Gospel Tract Foundation in Tucson, Arizona, claimed that on June 28, 1981, he and his followers, many of whom had given away money and possessions, would be lifted into heaven "like helium balloons" just before the Tribulation.

1789 In 1418, the French theologian, astrologer, and cardinal of the Roman Catholic Church Pierre d'Ailly wrote that the Book of Revelation seen through the lens of astronomical cycles presaged the coming of the Antichrist in 1789.

Late 18th Century Former lieutenant in the Royal Navy and self-proclaimed prophet Richard Brothers wrote in his 1792 book, *Revealed Knowledge of the Prophecies and Times*, that he was the "Prince of the Hebrews," that London was Babylon, and that the monarchies of the world would all soon fall, ushering in the millennium. In 1795, he was arrested for treason and imprisoned in an insane asylum where he purportedly spent the rest of his life designing flags and palaces for New Jerusalem.

JULY 2013?

1 MONDAY	**2** TUESDAY	**3** WEDNESDAY

NOTES

4 THURSDAY

5 FRIDAY

6 SATURDAY

7 SUNDAY

JULY 2013?

8 MONDAY

9 TUESDAY

10 WEDNESDAY

11 THURSDAY

NOTES

12 FRIDAY

13 SATURDAY

14 SUNDAY

1867 Church of Scotland clergyman and anti-Catholic preacher John Cumming believed that the French Revolution and the Irish potato famine fulfilled biblical prophecies. He preached that the "sixth vial of judgment" had been poured out in 1820 and that therefore Judgment Day would occur some time between 1848 and 1867.

1867 In his 1860 publication, *The Coming Battle and the Appalling National Convulsions Foreshown in Prophecy Immediately to Occur During the Period 1861–67*, English-born preacher Michael Paget Baxter claimed that Napoleon III was the Antichrist and that by 1866 "the awful calamities will commence that are to accompany Christ's Advent." Baxter would go on to predict the end of the world seven different times between 1867 and 1908.

JULY 2013?

15 MONDAY | **16** TUESDAY | **17** WEDNESDAY | **18** THURSDAY

July 15, 1967

In 1965, Reverend James Warren "Jim" Jones, civil rights activist, and founder and leader of the Peoples Temple, which is best known for the 1978 mass suicide of 909 of its members in Guyana, claimed that a global nuclear war would begin on July 15, 1967.

July 15, 1994

Polish-born and self-proclaimed nun, prophet and astronomer Sofia Richmond, or Sister Marie, produced numerous elaborate, full-page advertisements in British daily newspapers claiming that the Shoemaker-Levy 9 comet, already projected to strike Jupiter, was actually Halley's comet and that by July 15, 1994, this impact would create a "cosmic explosion" and a "gigantic fireball that would wipe out nations on Earth."

NOTES

19 FRIDAY

20 SATURDAY

21 SUNDAY

1873 In 1870, Pennsylvania Millerite preacher Jonas Wendell published a pamphlet titled *The Present Truth, or Meat in Due Season*, concluding that the Second Advent was to occur in 1873. He died in August of that year.

1873 Inventor and Millerite author Nelson Horatio Barbour published a pamphlet in 1871 titled *Evidences for the Coming of the Lord in 1873*. Hundreds gathered on Terry Island in Connecticut to await his predicted Advent of Christ.

JULY 2013?

22 MONDAY

23 TUESDAY

24 WEDNESDAY

25 THURSDAY

July 22, 1556
Popular rumor throughout Europe predicted the end of the world would come on July 22, 1556, when Magdalene's Day fell.

NOTES

26 FRIDAY

27 SATURDAY

28 SUNDAY

1878 In 1876, Nelson Horatio Barbour and Millerite-influenced preacher Charles Taze Russell, founder of the Bible Student movement from which the Jehovah's Witnesses would emerge, collaborated on the calculation that 1878 would be the year of the Second Coming.

1880 English theologian and professor of moral philosophy Thomas Rawson Birks claimed in his 1843 book, *First Elements of Sacred Prophecy: Including an Examination of Several Recent Expositions and of the Year-Day Theory*, that the restoration of Israel, as predicted in the Bible to presage the return of Christ, would occur no later than 1880.

JULY 2013?

29 MONDAY

30 TUESDAY

31 WEDNESDAY

1885 Welsh Protestant preacher Christopher Love, in his posthumously published *The Strange and Wonderful Predictions of Mr. Christopher Love*, prophesied earthquakes in 1779, wars in Germany and America in 1780, destruction of the Roman Catholic Church in 1790, the moon turning to blood in 1800, and a world-destroying earthquake in 1885. Love was executed for treason and conspiracy in the Presbyterian plot to restore Charles II.

Early 20th Century In 1918, shortly after the British capture of Jerusalem from the Ottoman Empire, a group of ten English clergymen published a short manifesto titled "The Significance of the Hour," in which they proclaimed a close to "the time of the Gentiles" and that the return of Christ could be expected at any moment.

1 THURSDAY

2 FRIDAY

3 SATURDAY

4 SUNDAY

AUGUST 2013?

5 MONDAY

6 TUESDAY

7 WEDNESDAY

8 THURSDAY

NOTES

9 FRIDAY

10 SATURDAY

11 SUNDAY

1900 Brazilian Christian mystic, religious leader, and onetime lawyer Antônio Conselheiro, "the Counselor," claimed "a great rain of stars" would end the world in 1900. A critic of the Catholic Church and the Brazilian government, Conselheiro founded the communal village of Bello Monte in 1893 on a large abandoned farm in northern Brazil. By 1895, its population had grown to more than 30,000, made up largely of landless farmers, former slaves, and indigenous people. Fearing the success of the growing autonomous region, the Brazilian military destroyed the town, killing more than 15,000 of the village's inhabitants.

AUGUST 2013?

12 MONDAY

13 TUESDAY

14 WEDNESDAY

15 THURSDAY

NOTES

16 FRIDAY

17 SATURDAY

18 SUNDAY

August 17, 1987
Artist, art historian, onetime Princeton professor, and popularizer of the Mayan calendar, José Argüelles, born Joseph Anthony Arguelles, suggested in the early 1980s that his planned Harmonic Convergence, in which thousands of people would gather on August 16 and 17, 1987, at sites around the world and "synchronize their vibrations," would prevent a "wobble that would tear the continents apart, or a nuclear war."

1911 Influential 19th-century Scottish astronomer Charles Piazzi Smyth, a pioneer of the practice of placing telescopes at high altitudes, made several predictions as to the date of the Second Coming based on his belief that his firsthand measurements of the Great Pyramid of Giza revealed secret prophecies built in its structure by the biblical Noah, who supervised its construction. Smyth first proposed 1882 and then several other dates between 1892 and 1911.

AUGUST 2013?

19 MONDAY

20 TUESDAY

21 WEDNESDAY

22 THURSDAY

August 20, 1953
In the 1940 edition of their book *The Great Pyramid: Its Divine Message*, English physician and pyramidologist Dr. Herbert Aldersmith and Scottish engineer David Davidson wrote that August 20, 1953, would be the "Armageddon Climax."

NOTES

23 FRIDAY

24 SATURDAY

25 SUNDAY

1914 Elliott Kenan Kamwana, a Nyasaland preacher who popularized the Jehovah's Witnesses teachings of Charles Taze Russell in present-day Malawi, Mozambique, and South Africa, believed that meteor showers and the outbreak of World War I were signs that Christ's Second Coming would happen in 1914. Kamwana also believed this event would expel all European colonialists from Africa.

1936 Early pioneer of radio and televangelism, and founder of the Worldwide Church of God and the Ambassador College in Pasadena, California, Herbert W. Armstrong made numerous predictions for the return of Christ over his career: 1936, October 1943, and 1957, as well as prophesying World War III for between 1971 and 1976.

AUGUST 2013?

26 MONDAY

27 TUESDAY

28 WEDNESDAY

29 THURSDAY

NOTES

30 FRIDAY

31 SATURDAY

1 SUNDAY

1947 In 1889, John Ballou Newbrough, American dentist, spiritualist, and founder of the religious commune Land of Shalam in Las Cruces, New Mexico, claimed that by 1947 "all the present governments, religions, and all monied monopolies are to be overthrown and to go out of existence."

1950s American author, pilot, self-proclaimed UFO contactee, host of the Giant Rock Spacecraft Convention, and founder of a UFO-focused community near Landers, California, George Van Tassel claimed that the extraterrestrial being Ashtar informed him of a "planetary cleansing" in the form of an imminent nuclear war to occur in the 1950s.

SEPTEMBER 2013?

2 MONDAY

3 TUESDAY

4 WEDNESDAY

5 THURSDAY

NOTES

6 FRIDAY

7 SATURDAY

8 SUNDAY

September 6, 1994
American preacher and Christian radio broadcaster Harold Egbert Camping announced in his book *1994?* that Judgment Day would occur on or about September 6, 1994.

1977 In 1933, Kentucky Pentecostal minister and self-proclaimed faith healer William Marrion Branham predicted "that 1977 ought to terminate the world systems and usher in the millennium."

1981 Charles Ward "Chuck" Smith, senior pastor and founder of the Christian megachurch Calvary Chapel in Costa Mesa, California (hub of the 1960s Jesus People youth movement), declared in his 1978 booklet, *End Times*, that Christ would return sometime before 1981.

SEPTEMBER 2013?

9 MONDAY

10 TUESDAY

11 WEDNESDAY

12 THURSDAY

NOTES

13 FRIDAY

14 SATURDAY

15 SUNDAY

September 13, 1988

In his best-selling book *88 Reasons Why the Rapture Will Be in 1988*, former NASA employee and Bible student Edgar C. Whisenant predicted the Rapture for Rosh Hashanah in 1988, or between September 11 and 13.

September 15, 1829

Johann George Rapp, mystic, self-proclaimed prophet, and religious émigré from Germany, predicted September 15, 1829, for the return of Christ. His sect, known as the Harmonites, Rappites, or the Harmony Society, established the profitable commune towns of Harmony and Economy, Pennsylvania.

1982 In his 1976 book, *When the Planets Align…(SYZYGY) Earthquake 1982!!*, Canadian religious author Doug Clark claimed Jesus would return in 1982 and rapture Christians away from global catastrophes he believed would come from that year's alignment of planets.

1982 In 1980, Marion Gordon "Pat" Robertson, televangelist and founder of the Christian Broadcasting Network, claimed during a broadcast of *The 700 Club*, "I guarantee you by the end of 1982 there is going to be a judgment on the world."

SEPTEMBER 2013?

16 MONDAY

17 TUESDAY

18 WEDNESDAY

19 THURSDAY

NOTES

20 FRIDAY

21 SATURDAY

22 SUNDAY

1986 In 1968 in Huntington Beach, California, David Brandt Berg, also known as Moses David, founded the Children of God, famous for its practice of "flirty fishing," or using female members to seduce new converts. One of Berg's many predictions claimed that the Antichrist and his "one world government" would begin their "reign of terror" in 1986.

1997 American religious leader of the New Age group Heaven's Gate Marshall Herff Applewhite made two major claims: that he was a reincarnation of Jesus Christ and that an alien spaceship was trailing the Hale-Bopp comet. He and his 39 followers committed mass suicide on March 26, 1997, in order to "evacuate earth," avoid its imminent "recycling," and ascend to an "above human" existence aboard the alien ship.

SEPTEMBER 2013?

23 MONDAY

24 TUESDAY

25 WEDNESDAY

26 THURSDAY

September 23, 1186
In 1184, Iberian astrologers circulated the Letter of Toledo, and caused panic throughout Europe. It warned that the world was going to be destroyed on September 23, 1186, by storms, famine, pestilence, and earthquake due to a rare alignment of the planets.

27 FRIDAY

28 SATURDAY

29 SUNDAY

September 28, 1992
Born-again Christian Rollen Frederick Stewart, also known as Rock 'n' Rollen and famous for wearing a rainbow wig and holding up "John 3:16" signs at sporting events, believed the Rapture would take place on September 28, 1992. In order to "get the message out," Rollen held a person hostage in a Los Angeles hotel six days prior.

1997 In 1992, Shoko Asahara, leader of the Japanese religious group Aum Shinrikyo, declared himself Christ and Japan's only fully enlightened master. Asahara also prophesied that the United States would instigate a nuclear Armageddon in 1997. In 1995, in an attempt to divert police attention away from the group, Aum members carried out a sarin gas attack in the Tokyo subway, killing 13 commuters, seriously injuring 54, and affecting at least 980 more.

1998 In the early 20th century, American self-proclaimed psychic Edgar Cayce, one of the seminal figures in the birth of the modern New Age movement, with its belief in an imminent purification or spiritual transformation of humanity and the earth, prophesied the "entrance of the Messiah" and catastrophic "earth changes," including a polar reversal, for year 1998.

30 MONDAY

1 TUESDAY

2 WEDNESDAY

October 1, 1914
Millerite-influenced preacher Charles Taze Russell's second prediction for the return of Christ was based on his revised biblical chronology combined with his belief that the Great Pyramid of Giza was built by the Hebrews and contained prophecies hidden in its geometry. Following October 1, 1914, Russell claimed that Jesus' return had been invisible.

NOTES

3 THURSDAY

4 FRIDAY

5 SATURDAY

6 SUNDAY

OCTOBER 2013?

7 MONDAY

8 TUESDAY

9 WEDNESDAY

10 THURSDAY

NOTES

11 FRIDAY

12 SATURDAY

13 SUNDAY

October 13, 1736
William Whiston, controversial English theologian, historian, and onetime professor of mathematics at the University of Cambridge, predicted a comet would destroy the world on October 13, 1736.

October 1978
In his 1973 book, *The Doomsday Globe*, Australian author and businessman John Strong used pyramidology and biblical chronology to predict global nuclear war for October 1978, prompting him and 70 followers to build bomb shelters on a ranch 400 miles northwest of Sydney.

Late 20th Century In 1981, James Watt, Secretary of the Interior under Ronald Reagan, told Congress, "I don't know how many future generations we can count on until the Lord returns" in response to questions regarding environmental conservation.

Late 20th Century American author Mary Stewart Relfe's 1981 book, *The New Money System*, claimed that God communicated to her in her dreams that the Second Coming was imminent. Relfe also originated the now-widespread belief that the then-new Universal Product Codes were the "mark of the beast" prophesied by the apostle John in the Book of Revelation.

14 MONDAY

15 TUESDAY

16 WEDNESDAY

17 THURSDAY

October 14, 2000
Founder and religious leader of the Texas-based, Judaism-inspired House of Yahweh, Yisrayl Hawkins (aka "Buffalo" Bill Hawkins) proclaimed that the Israeli peace accord signed in 1993 started a seven-year period of tribulation that would end on October 14, 2000, with the "return of the Yeshua," or Messiah. Hawkins would go on also to predict a global nuclear war for September 12, 2006.

18 FRIDAY

19 SATURDAY

20 SUNDAY

October 19, 1533
German monk and mathematician Michael Stifel calculated from the Book of Revelation that Judgment Day would begin at 8 a.m. on October 19, 1533.

October 19, 1814
English religious mystic and self-describe d prophetess Joanna Southcott made two unfulfilled predictions: "Pregnant" at the age of 64, she would give birth to the new Messiah on October 19, 1814, and the Day of Judgment would come in the year 2004. She died of dropsy in December 1814.

Late 20th Century In 1984, Indian mystic, guru, spiritual teacher, and founder of the 7,000-member intentional community Rajneeshpuram in Wasco County, Oregon, Bhagwan Shree Rajneesh (born Chandra Mohan Jain), prophesied that two-thirds of humanity would die of AIDS by the end of the century. Also in 1984, Rajneesh was implicated in the intentional salmonella poisoning, carried out by his followers, of 751 residents of a neighboring town in what is now known as the first bioterrorist attack in United States' history.

OCTOBER 2013?

21 MONDAY

22 TUESDAY

23 WEDNESDAY

24 THURSDAY

October 22, 1844
Samuel S. Snow, a former skeptic turned Millerite preacher, predicted the Second Coming, or Advent, for "the tenth day of the seventh month of the present year, 1844," which he converted to October 22, 1844, using the Karaite Jewish calendar. After its passing, this day became known as the Great Disappointment.

October 23, 1997
Seventeenth-century Irish archbishop James Ussher's interpretation of biblical chronology led him to claim that the world would end on the 6,000th anniversary of creation, or October 23, 1997.

25 FRIDAY

26 SATURDAY

27 SUNDAY

2000 South Korean billionaire, world political power broker, religious leader, and founder of the Unification Church,—which claims five to seven million members worldwide—Reverend Sun Myung Moon proclaimed in 1977 that the "principle of restoration through indemnity" indicated that Christ's Second Coming would be in the year 2000.

2001 In 1980, Unarius Academy of Science member Louis "Charles" Spiegel predicted that in 2001 a fleet of 33 mile-long alien spaceships would land at its compound in El Cajon, California, signaling the end of the world. The Universal, Articulate, Interdimensional Understanding of Science (Unarius) Academy of Science was founded in 1954 by Ernest Norman, a self-proclaimed psychic and reincarnation of Jesus Christ, who preached that Asiatic peoples were descended from Martians.

28 MONDAY

29 TUESDAY

30 WEDNESDAY

31 THURSDAY

October 28, 1992
Thousands of South Koreans prepared for the Hyoo-Go, or Rapture, after Lee Jang-rim, leader of the Mission for the Coming Days, predicted he and his followers would be lifted to heaven before pestilence swept the earth on October 28, 1992.
Lee was convicted of fraud after it was found that he had bought bonds with maturities extending beyond October 28.

NOTES

1 FRIDAY

2 SATURDAY

3 SUNDAY

2001 In the 1980s, high-ranking member and writer for the Nation of Islam Tynetta Muhammad predicted through her numerological analysis of the Bible and Koran that Ronald Reagan was the Antichrist and that a racial world war and a global fire lasting 390 years would begin in 2001, destroying the Caucasian race. A fleet of "divine spaceships" would arrive just prior to the final conflagration to rescue the faithful.

2006 American journalist and author Michael Drosnin suggested in his 1997 book, *Bible Code,* that the Bible was written by aliens and contains a code that he could use to predict significant future events, including a nuclear holocaust occurring between 1998 and 2006.

NOVEMBER 2013?

4 MONDAY	**5** TUESDAY	**6** WEDNESDAY	**7** THURSDAY

NOTES

8 FRIDAY

9 SATURDAY

10 SUNDAY

November 10, 1993
In 1990, Russian New Age religious leader of the Great White Brotherhood Maria Devi Christos, born Marina Tsvigun, predicted the "Time of Apocalypses" for November 10, 1993. Christos referred to herself as the "Moshiah of Jews, the Ardhanarishvara of the Tantriests, the Akmat (White Mother) of the Moslems, the Maitraya of the Buddhists, and the Sophia of the Slavs."

2007 During a January 2007 broadcast of *The 700 Club*, media mogul and television evangelist Marion Gordon "Pat" Robertson announced that God had spoken to him and told him that "mass killings" from a terrorist attack on the United States would occur in 2007. He added, "The Lord didn't say nuclear. But I do believe it will be something like that."

11 MONDAY

12 TUESDAY

13 WEDNESDAY

14 THURSDAY

November 11, 2011
Solara Antara Amaa-ra, New Age leader of the 11:11 Doorway movement, claimed that she, along with 144,000 believers worldwide, opened a cosmic spiritual portal on January 11, 1992, that needed to be entered before it closed on November 11, 2011, if one was to avoid being trapped in a "dualistic existence" and instead "shift evolutionary spirals and ascend into Oneness."

NOTES

15 FRIDAY

16 SATURDAY

17 SUNDAY

2012 Numerous Internet sources predicted the year 2012 for the end of the world caused by a variety of imminent destructive natural forces, including a super solar storm, a supernova, a super volcano, an interplanetary alignment, earth's magnetic poles switching, and a collision with a stellar object such as a brown dwarf, a black hole, a giant asteroid, or an errant planet called Nibiru. There are also theories of a man-made doomsday, intentionally initiated by the American High Frequency Active Auroral Research Program (HAARP), an ionospheric-research program.

2012 In his 2002 book, *The Orion Prophecy: Will the World Be Destroyed in 2012?*, New Age author Patrick Geryl predicted that in the year 2012 gigantic solar flares would reverse the magnetic polarity of the earth, causing massive earthquakes and tsunamis, and triggering intense volcanic activity and continental drift, killing nearly all of humanity.

NOVEMBER 2013?

18 MONDAY

19 TUESDAY

20 WEDNESDAY

21 THURSDAY

NOTES

22 FRIDAY

23 SATURDAY

24 SUNDAY

2035 French former journalist and founder of the atheist, UFO-focused Raëlian Church, Raël, born Claude Vorilhon, claimed that in 1973 aliens called Elohim took him aboard their spaceship, hidden in an extinct volcano in central France, and revealed to him that they had scientifically created life on earth and that they had later bred with human women to create the ancient Hebrews. Raël also predicted that in 2035 the Elohim would return to earth, landing at the Raëlian "extraterrestrial embassy" in Israel, to usher in an apocalypse, with the Raëlians' minds being physically transferred into cloned, disease-free bodies.

NOVEMBER 2013?

25 MONDAY	**26** TUESDAY	**27** WEDNESDAY	**28** THURSDAY

29 FRIDAY

30 SATURDAY

1 SUNDAY

2100 Scientists claim that the influence of human behavior on the earth's ecosystems through deforestation, mineral extraction, hunting, pollution, urbanization, and the introduction of nonnative species would result in the extinction of one-half of earth's higher life-forms by 2100.

DECEMBER 2013?

2 MONDAY

3 TUESDAY

4 WEDNESDAY

5 THURSDAY

NOTES

6 FRIDAY

7 SATURDAY

8 SUNDAY

2900 Azerbaijani-born American author and "ancient astronaut" proponent Zecharia Sitchin claimed in his 2007 book, *The End of Days*, that ancient Sumerian texts reveal that a planet called Nibiru passes near Earth every 3,600 years and allows its alien inhabitants to interact with humanity. Sitchin predicted the return of Nibiru for sometime around 2900. Sitchin also claimed that ancient aliens crossed extraterrestrial genes with those of *Homo erectus* to genetically engineer the human race to be slaves in their gold mines.

1,000,000,000 Scientists predict that in one billion years the sun will be 11 percent brighter than it is now, creating a runaway greenhouse effect, raising temperatures enough to evaporate all of earth's water, and ending multicellular life.

DECEMBER 2013?

9 MONDAY

10 TUESDAY

11 WEDNESDAY

12 THURSDAY

NOTES

13 FRIDAY

14 SATURDAY

15 SUNDAY

4,000,000,000 According to scientists, in four billion years from now our galaxy will collide with the Andromeda galaxy, possibly dislodging our solar system from its current position.

7,900,000,000 Scientis speculate that in 7.9 billion years from now our sun will swell into a red giant star, swallowing Mercury, Venus, and possibly Earth.

DECEMBER 2013?

16 MONDAY

17 TUESDAY

18 WEDNESDAY

19 THURSDAY

NOTES

20 FRIDAY

21 SATURDAY

22 SUNDAY

December 21, 1954
Fifty-four-year-old Chicago housewife Dorothy Martin claimed that aliens from the planet Clarion told her the world would end before dawn on December 21, 1954, but that she and her faithful associates—many of whom had left jobs, college, and spouses, and had given away money and possessions—would be saved by space-ships. In 1955, under the threat of institutionalization, Martin left Chicago, spending several years in the Peruvian Andes, returning to the U.S. in the 1960s as Sister Thedra.

December 21, 2012
Numerous New Age authors and practitioners claimed that the last day of the Mayan calendar was December 21, 2012, and that this date would be the beginning of a global purification and transformation precipitated by alien visitation and/or spiritual enlightenment and/or our evolution into noncorporeal beings and/ or the apocalypse.

50,000,000,000 If the universe's expansion continues to accelerate infinitely it would result in what some scientists refer to as the "big rip", where gravitational, electromagnetic and weak nuclear forces are overwhelmed, resulting in the tearing apart of galaxies, stars and eventually atoms themselves 35 to 50 billion years from now.

DECEMBER 2013?

23 MONDAY

24 TUESDAY

25 WEDNESDAY

26 THURSDAY

December 23, 2012
The alternative date for the completion of the Mayan calendar was December 23, 2012, which was supported by a smaller number of New Age authors and practitioners.

NOTES

27 FRIDAY

28 SATURDAY

29 SUNDAY

100,000,000,000 If the universe's expansion is not infinite it might slow and even reverse itself, causing space and time to collapse back into a singularity 100 billion years from now, in what some scientists call the "big crunch".

100,000,000,000 Some scientists have asserted that in 100 billion years from now the "big crunch" may be followed by another big bang in what is a cyclic or oscillatory model of the universe known as the "big bounce".

30 MONDAY

31 TUESDAY

1 WEDNESDAY

December 31, 1999
Catholic minister and leader of the Ugandan religious group called the Movement for the Restoration of the Ten Commandments of God, Joseph Kibweteere predicted that the world would end on December 31, 1999. Within three months of his failed prediction, Kibweteere, along with other leaders of his movement, would murder 778 of his followers through poisoning, strangulation, and setting fire to their church after boarding 530 members up inside.

NOTES

100,000,000,000,000 Many scientists, believing that the universe will expand infinitely, predict it will eventually become too cold in 100 trillion years for star formation or the transformation of matter and energy, resulting in what scientists call the "big freeze", leaving behind only white and brown dwarfs, neutron stars, and black holes.

2 THURSDAY

3 FRIDAY

4 SATURDAY

5 SUNDAY

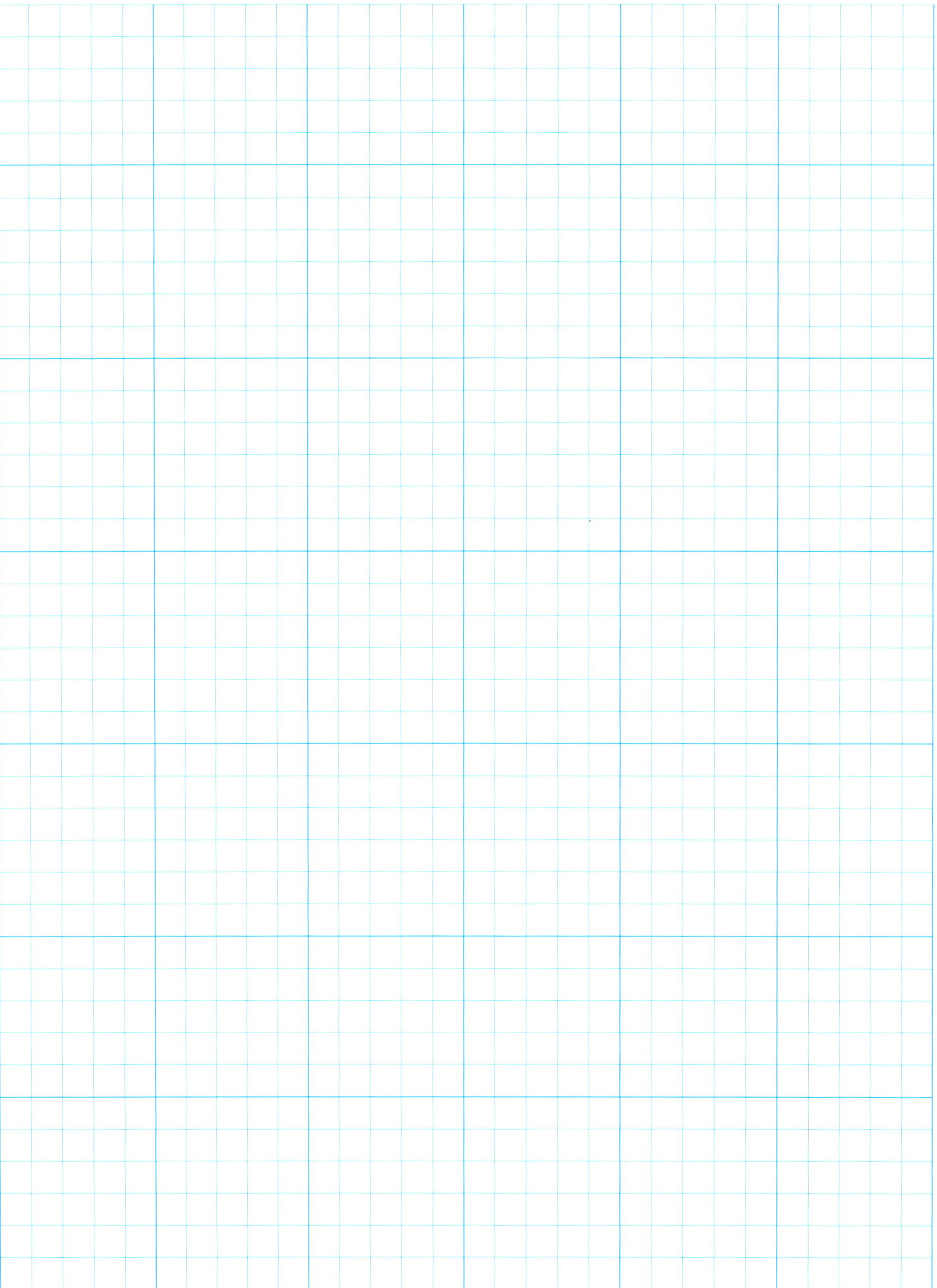

INTERNATIONAL HOLIDAYS

JAN 1	NEW YEAR'S DAY
JAN 7	CHRISTMAS (Eastern Orthodox)
JAN 21	MARTIN LUTHER KING JR. DAY
JAN 24	MILAD-UN-NABI (Prophet's Birthday)
JAN 27	INT'L HOLOCAUST REMEMBRANCE DAY
FEB 1	NATIONAL FREEDOM DAY (U.S.)
FEB 9	TÊT (Vietnamese New Year)
FEB 10	CHUNJIÉ (Chinese New Year)
FEB 12	SHROVE TUESDAY
FEB 12	MARDI GRAS
FEB 13	ASH WEDNESDAY
FEB 14	VALENTINE'S DAY
FEB 15	PARINIRVANA DAY
FEB 18	PRESIDENTS' DAY
FEB 20	WORLD DAY OF SOCIAL JUSTICE
FEB 21	INT'L MOTHER LANGUAGE DAY
MAR 08	INTERNATIONAL WOMEN'S DAY
MAR 10	DAYLIGHT SAVING TIME BEGINS
MAR 14	PI (π) DAY
MAR 17	ST. PATRICK'S DAY
MAR 20	MARCH EQUINOX
MAR 21	NOWRUZ (Persian New Year)
MAR 26	PASSOVER BEGINS
MAR 31	EASTER
APR 1	APRIL FOOL'S DAY
APR 4	TOMB SWEEPING DAY (China)
APR 15	TAX DAY (U.S.)
APR 22	EARTH DAY
APR 24	ARMENIAN GENOCIDE REMEMBRANCE DAY
MAY 1	MAY DAY/LABOUR DAY
MAY 5	CINCO DE MAYO
MAY 9	VICTORY IN EUROPE OVER FASCISM DAY
MAY 12	MOTHER'S DAY
MAY 24	VESAK (Buddha's Birthday)
MAY 25	AFRICAN LIBERATION DAY
MAY 27	MEMORIAL DAY (U.S.)
JUNE 16	FATHER'S DAY
JUNE 21	JUNE SOLSTICE
JULY 4	INDEPENDENCE DAY (U.S.)
JULY 6	JAN HUS DAY (Czech Republic)
JULY 9	RAMADAN BEGINS
JULY 14	BASTILLE DAY (France)
AUG 9	WORLD INDIGENOUS PEOPLES' DAY
AUG 15	FLOODING OF THE NILE (Egypt)
AUG 29	INT'L DAY AGAINST NUCLEAR TESTS
SEP 2	LABOR DAY (U.S.)
SEP 5	ROSH HASHANA (Jewish New Year)
SEP 14	YOM KIPPUR
SEP 21	INTERNATIONAL DAY OF PEACE
SEP 22	SEPTEMBER EQUINOX
SEP 29	GOLD STAR MOTHER'S DAY
OCT 1	NATIONAL DAY OF THE PEOPLE'S REPUBLIC OF CHINA
OCT 14	COLUMBUS DAY
OCT 14	INDIGENOUS PEOPLE'S DAY
OCT 14	THANKSGIVING DAY (Canada)
OCT 31	HALLOWEEN
NOV 1	DAY OF THE DEAD
NOV 3	DAYLIGHT SAVING TIME ENDS
NOV 5	AL-HIJRA (Islamic New Year)
NOV 11	VETERANS' DAY
NOV 28	HANUKKAH BEGINS
NOV 28	THANKSGIVING DAY (U.S.)
DEC 21	DECEMBER SOLSTICE
DEC 25	CHRISTMAS DAY
DEC 26	KWANZAA BEGINS
DEC 31	NEW YEAR'S EVE

INTERNATIONAL DIALING CODES

AFGHANISTAN **93**

ALBANIA **355**

ALGERIA **213**

AMERICAN SAMOA **684**

ANGOLA **244**

ANTARCTICA **672**

ANTIGUA **268**

ARGENTINA **54**

ARMENIA **374**

ARUBA **297**

ASCENSION **247**

AUSTRALIA **61**

AUSTRIA **43**

AZERBAIJAN **994**

BAHAMAS **242**

BAHRAIN **973**

BANGLADESH **880**

BARBADOS **246**

BELGIUM **32**

BELIZE **501**

BERMUDA **441**

BHUTAN **975**

BOLIVIA **591**

BOSNIA AND
HERZEGOVINA **387**

BOTSWANA **267**

BRAZIL **55**

BRITISH VIRGIN
ISLANDS **284**

BULGARIA **359**

BURKINA FASO **226**

BURUNDI **257**

CAMBODIA **855**

CAMEROON **237**

CANADA **1**

CAYMAN ISLANDS **345**

CENTRAL AFRICAN
REPUBLIC **236**

CHAD REPUBLIC **235**

CHILE **56**

CHINA **86**

CHRISTMAS ISLAND **61**

COLOMBIA **57**

CONGO **242**

COSTA RICA **506**

CROATIA **385**

CUBA **53**

CYPRUS **357**

CZECH REPUBLIC **420**

DENMARK **45**

DJIBOUTI **253**

DOMINICA **767**

DOMINICAN
REP. **809**

EAST TIMOR **670**

EASTER ISLAND **56**

ECUADOR **593**

EGYPT **20**

EL SALVADOR **503**

EQUATORIAL GUINEA **240**

ERITREA **291**

ESTONIA **372**

ETHIOPIA **251**

FALKLAND ISLANDS **500**

FIJI ISLANDS **679**

FINLAND **358**

FRANCE **33**

FRENCH ANTILLES **596**

FRENCH GUIANA **594**

FRENCH POLYNESIA **689**

GABON REPUBLIC **241**

GAMBIA **220**

GEORGIA **995**

GERMANY **49**

GHANA **233**

GIBRALTAR **350**

GREECE **30**

GREENLAND **299**

GRENADA **473**

GUAM **671**

GUANTANAMO BAY **5399**

GUATEMALA **502**

GUYANA **592**

HAITI **509**

HONDURAS **504**

HONG KONG **852**

HUNGARY **36**

ICELAND **354**

INDIA **91**

INDONESIA **62**

IRAN **98**

IRAQ **964**

IRELAND **353**

ISLE OF MAN **44**

ISRAEL **972**

ITALY **39**

IVORY COAST **225**

JAMAICA **876**

JAPAN **81**

JORDAN **962**

KAZAKHSTAN **7**

KENYA **254**

KOREA, NORTH **850**

KOREA, SOUTH **82**

KOSOVO **381**

KUWAIT **965**

KYRGYZSTAN **996**

LAOS **856**

LATVIA **371**

LEBANON **961**

LIBERIA **231**

LIBYA **218**

LIECHTENSTEIN **423**

LITHUANIA **370**

LUXEMBOURG **352**

MACAU **853**

MACEDONIA **389**

MADAGASCAR **261**

MALAWI **265**

MALAYSIA **60**

MALDIVES **960**

MALI REPUBLIC **223**

MALTA **356**

MARSHALL ISLANDS **692**

MARTINIQUE **596**

MAURITIUS **230**

MEXICO **52**

MICRONESIA **691**

MIDWAY ISLANDS **808**

MOLDOVA **373**

MONACO **377**

MONGOLIA **976**

MONTSERRAT **664**

MOROCCO **212**

MOZAMBIQUE **258**

MYANMAR **95**

NAMIBIA **264**

NEPAL **977**

NETHERLANDS **31**

NEW CALEDONIA **687**

NEW ZEALAND **64**

NICARAGUA **505**

NIGER REPUBLIC **227**

NIGERIA **234**

NORFOLK ISLAND **672**

NORWAY **47**

PAKISTAN **92**

PANAMA **507**

PAPUA NEW GUINEA **675**

PARAGUAY **595**

PERU **51**

PHILIPPINES **63**

POLAND **48**

PORTUGAL **351**

PUERTO RICO **787**

QATAR **974**

ROMANIA **40**

RUSSIA **7**

RWANDA **250**

SAIPAN **670**

SAUDI ARABIA **966**

SENEGAL REPUBLIC **221**

SERBIA, REPUBLIC OF **381**

SEYCHELLES **248**

SIERRA LEONE **232**

SINGAPORE **65**

SLOVAKIA **421**

SLOVENIA **386**

SOLOMON ISLANDS **677**

SOMALIA REPUBLIC **252**

SOUTH AFRICA **27**

SPAIN **34**

SRI LANKA **94**

SUDAN **249**

SWAZILAND **268**

SWEDEN **46**

SWITZERLAND **41**

SYRIA **963**

TAIWAN **886**

TAJIKISTAN **992**

TANZANIA **255**

THAILAND **66**

TONGA **676**

TRINIDAD **868**

TUNISIA **216**

TURKEY **90**

TURKMENISTAN **993**

UGANDA **256**

UKRAINE **380**

UNITED ARAB
EMIRATES **971**

UNITED KINGDOM **44**

UNITED STATES **1**

URUGUAY **598**

US VIRGIN ISLANDS **340**

UZBEKISTAN **998**

VANUATU **678**

VATICAN CITY **39**

VENEZUELA **58**

VIETNAM **84**

YEMEN **967**

YUGOSLAVIA **381**

ZAIRE **243**

ZAMBIA **260**

ZANZIBAR **255**

ZIMBABWE **263**

TIME ZONES

-11 -10 -9 -8 -7 -6 -5 -4 -3 -2 -1 UTC +1 +2 +3 +4 +5 +6 +7 +8 +9 +10 +11 +12
HONOLULU
ANCHORAGE
LOS ANGELES
DENVER
CHICAGO, MEXICO CITY
NEW YORK CITY
CARACAS
RIO DE JANEIRO
FERNANDO DE NORONHA
AZORES
LONDON, LISBON, ABIDJAN
ROME, BERLIN, PARIS
ATHENS, CAPE TOWN
BAGHDAD, NAIROBI
DUBAI
MUMBAI
KATHMANDU
BANGKOK
HONG KONG
SEOUL, TOKYO
SYDNEY
SOLOMON ISLANDS
AUCKLAND

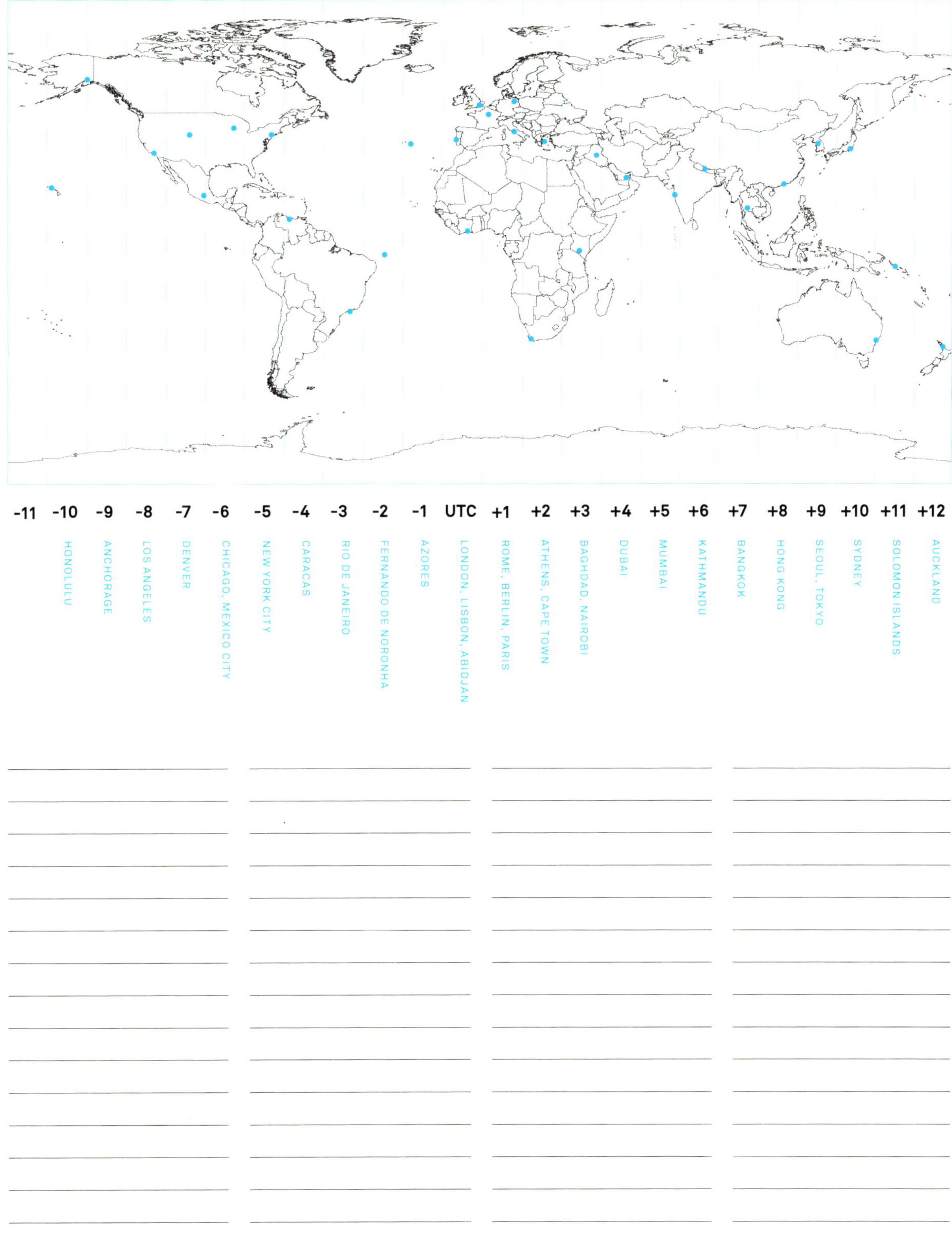

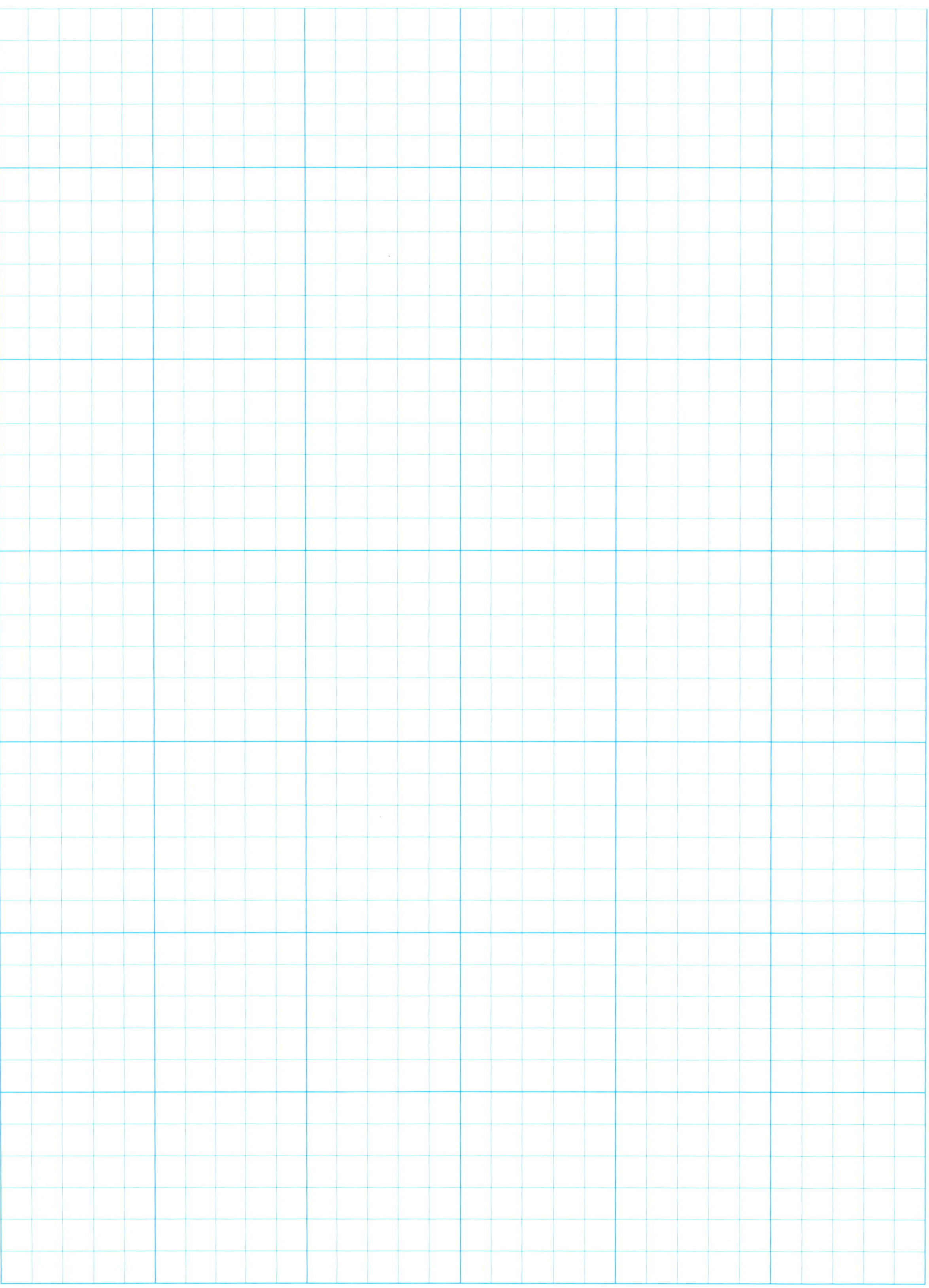

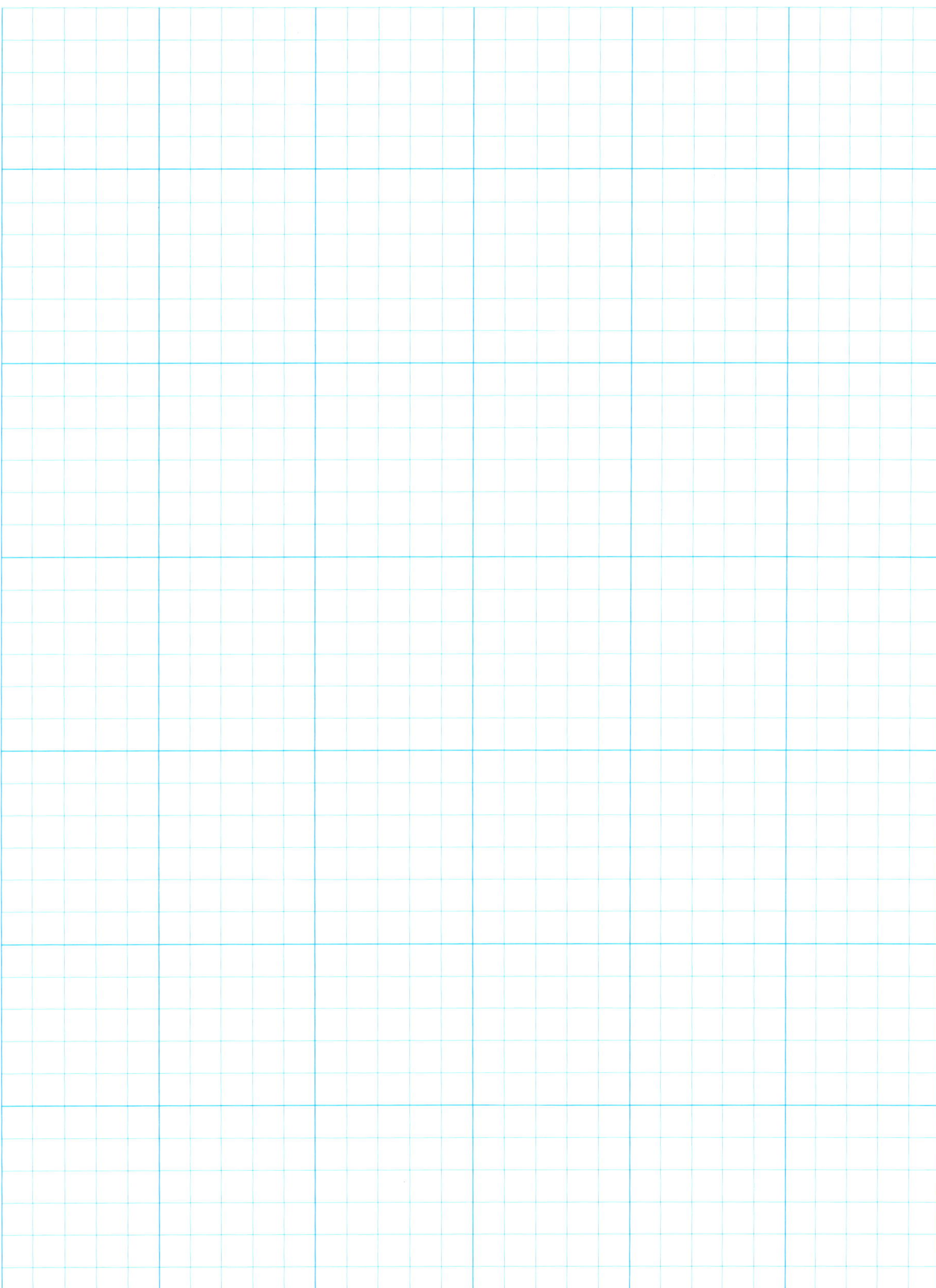

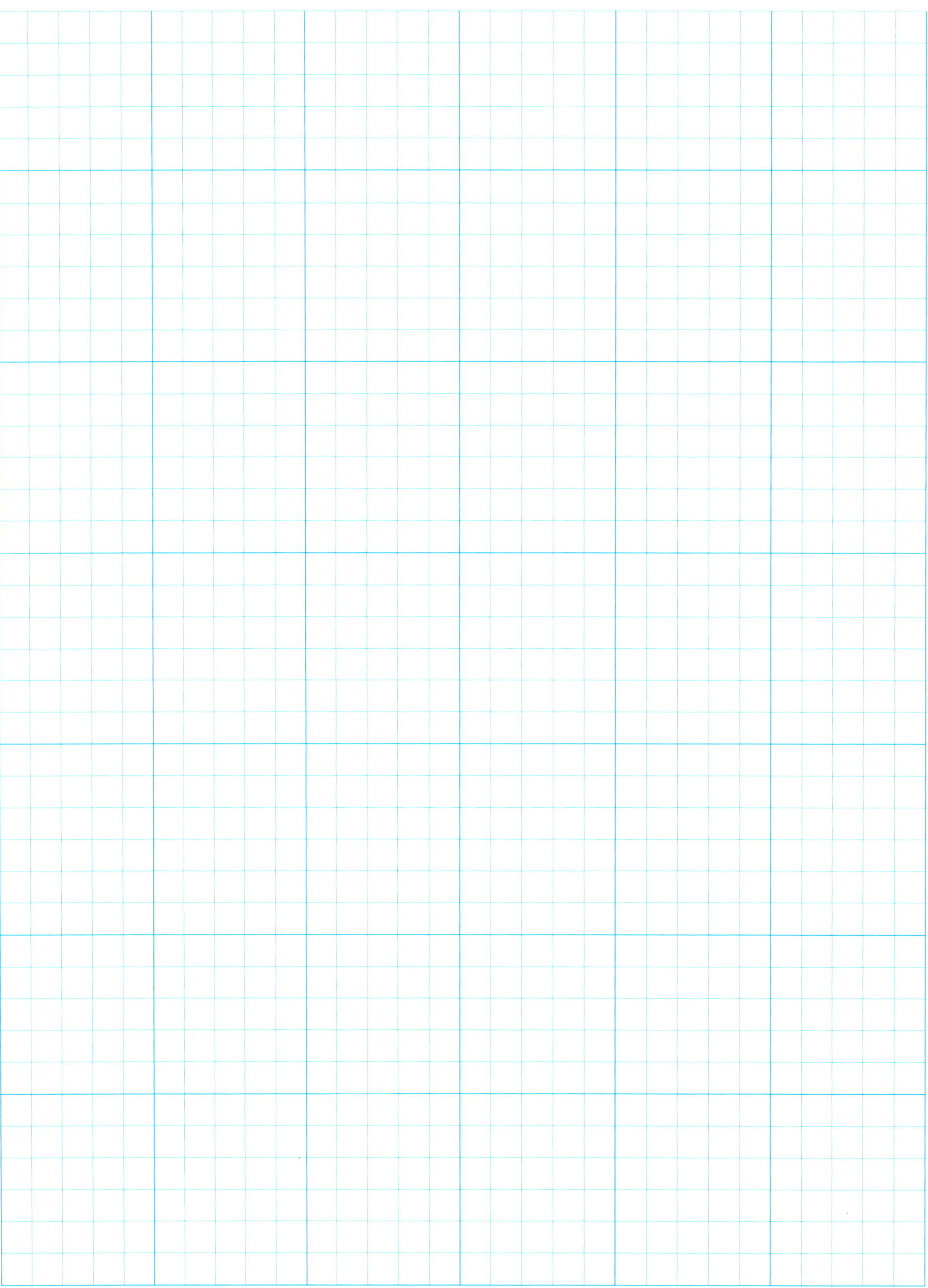

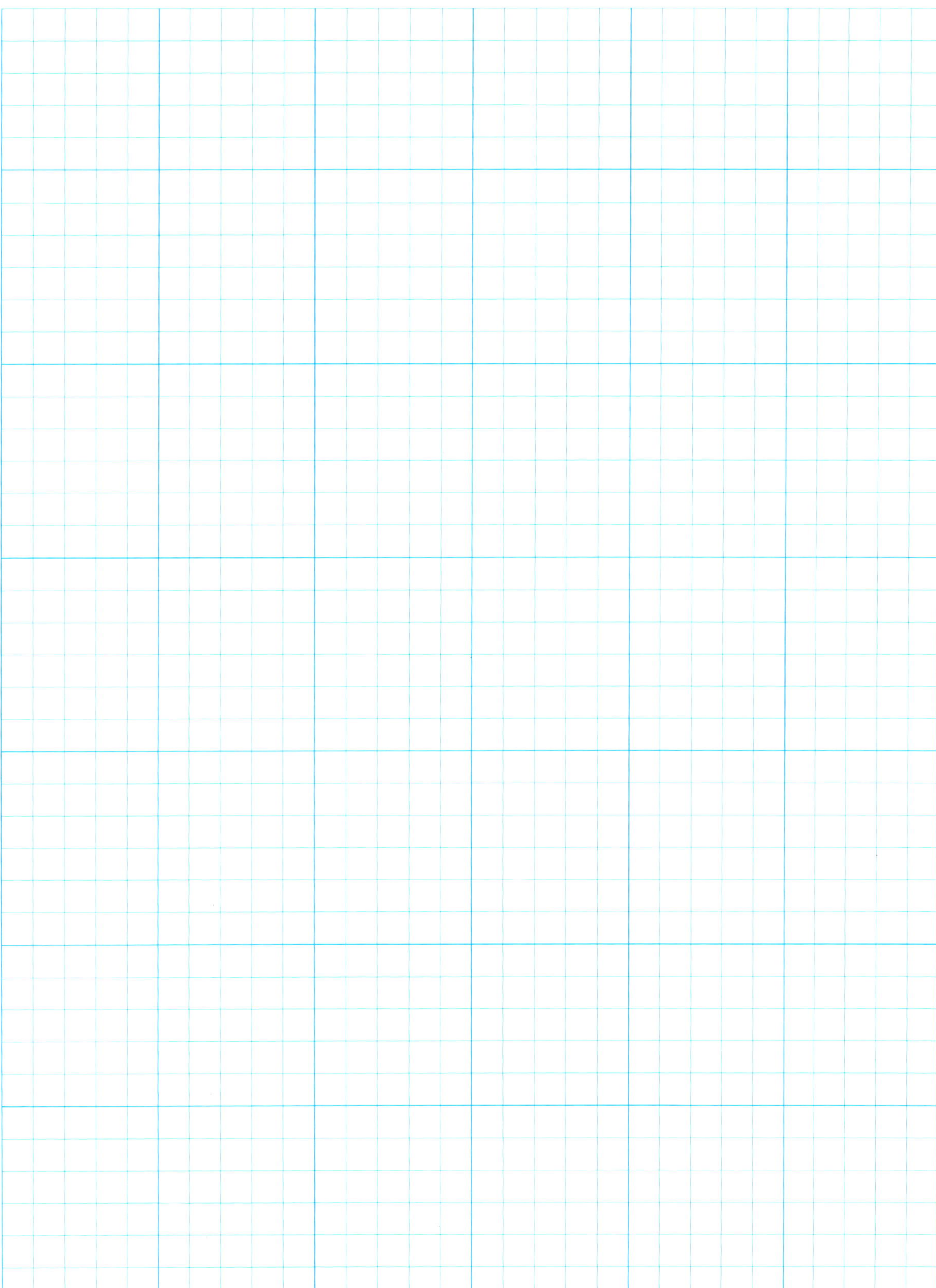

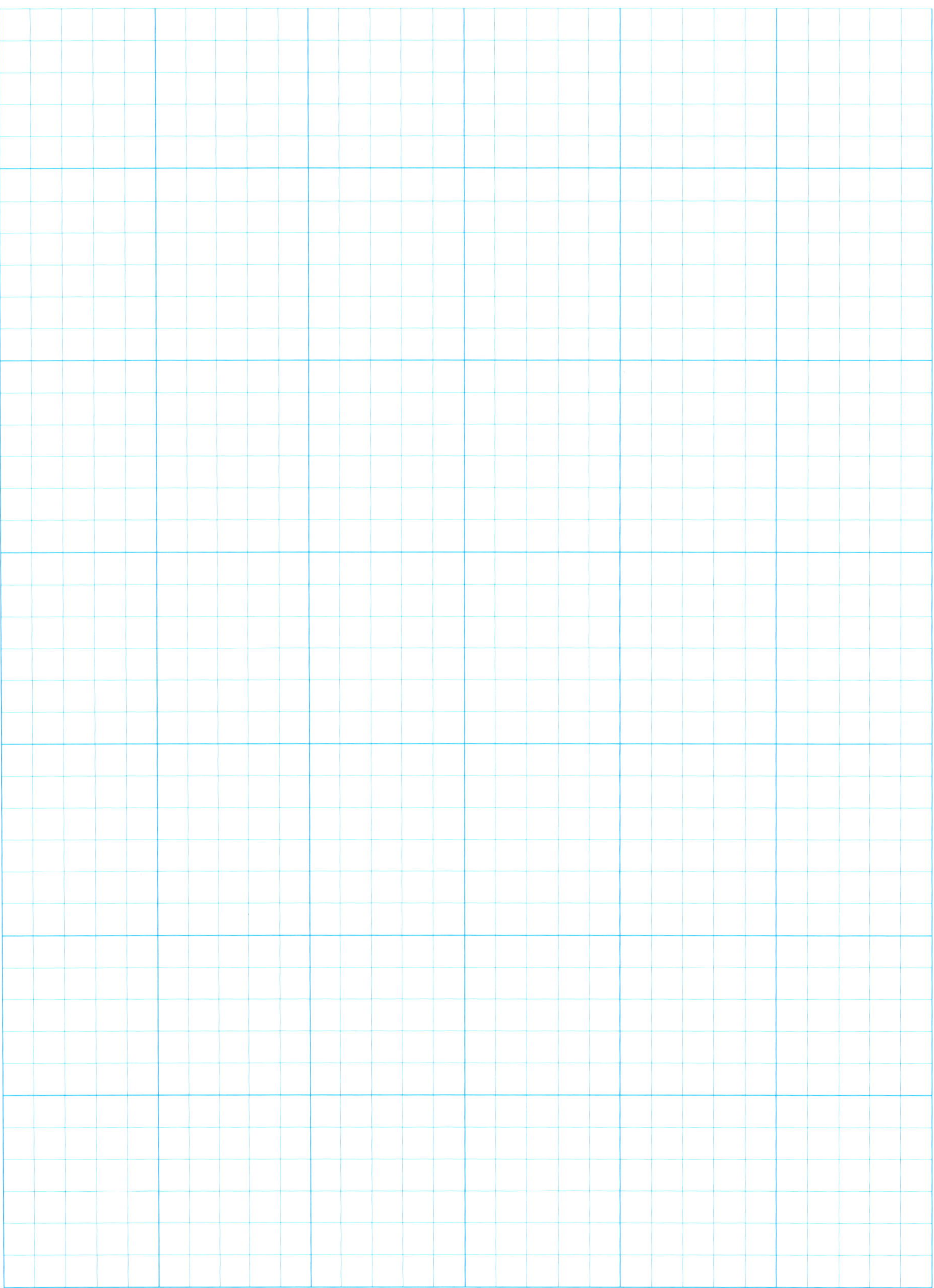

"I decline to accept the end of man."
— William Faulkner